Half a Man

Bill Glose

General Myers,
With gratitude for your
Kind words and your service
to our country,
Bill Glose

FUTURECYCLE PRESS

www.futurecycle.org

Published by FutureCycle Press
Hayesville, North Carolina, USA

ISBN 978-1-938853-49-4

for anyone touched by war

Contents

I

II

I

Half a Man

Head canted back, resting
on a pillow of sand. Just like
sleeping. Except for empty
eye sockets, flies skittering
in and out of his nose.
No meat below his sternum
only a knobby string of spine
pointing at us, accusingly.
We stood in a half-circle,
willing our eyes
to be just as lifeless.
"Fuck him," someone said.
"He would've done
the same to you." True,
or not, nothing more
to say. Carry on,
form a wedge, kick dunes
with desert boots,
search for someone to blame.

Search Team

The boys didn't know, thought
death was about to swing
its hammer at their heads.
Tears scythed through dust
caked on cheeks. Every lesson
had taught them men with guns
will take and take and take
then give back with the butt
of a rifle. Or its muzzle.

One soldier pointed his M-16
at the boys while another
said, "Ala-ess-fell"—
"down" in Arabic.
Bodies rattled like brown leaves
raked by winter's breath.

Hands scooped pockets, patted
dishdasha's white cotton.
Thumbs-up to his buddy
before lifting children, sending
them to their mother. Then on
to the next family huddled
against the adobe wall.

Desert Moon

Heat of the day. Men hunch over
weapon components spread on ponchos,

fussing like old women at a flea market.
Some nap beneath haloes of buzzing flies.

I lean against my rucksack on the side of a dune
tasting the sweet stillness. Undulating landscape

before me as strange as that of the desert moon,
pockmarked with craters from blows it never

anticipates. Specialist Taylor shows me
laminated photos of his baby girl. She lives

in the webbing of his Kevlar helmet. One day
he hopes to touch her face for real. Tefertiller

is writing home, pen perched in the corner
of his mouth like a swimmer on blocks

waiting for a gun to fire. Rambali shakes
a Tupperware with a scorpion inside. Pincers open,

wait for lid's burp, aching to snap at something soft.
Garner offers an MRE ham slice to a stray dog

thin as a tee shirt on a hanger. It sniffs, skittish,
as if it knows that next week shrapnel will

tattoo its name across Garner's stomach.
His heels will dig tiny graves in sand

while Gomez starts an IV. For now, though,
the dog takes the meat, Garner smiles, and

the desert moon inches across a cerulean sky.

Clearing a Room

"Clearing a room" sounds courteous,
inconsequential, so much like
clearing a table as if the term could steady
your hands, allow you to rush into
a room smiling, as if what you're doing
is as simple as searching for dirty napkins,
removing dinner plates. But no one
ever lost his legs bussing silverware.

Do antiseptic terms fool anyone?
Not the brass, who spoon them
like strained veggies to a teething child;
nor media, who pick at statistics
like tender scabs; but maybe mothers
ensconced in recliners, heating pads
pressed to smalls of backs, frightened
by what the nightly news might bring.

For them, "movement to contact"
connotes beef-fed boys marching
on manicured parade fields, white gloves
saluting. Because truth repulses.
Who wants news of tired men scurrying
over open sand with only smoke
to ward off flying steel? Jabbing
at bee's nests with bayonets to see
what flies out. Truth must be sanitized
before consumption.

To "clear a room," men form lines
and cascade past one another.
Luck lingers in the rear where comrades
in "overwatch" promise vengeance
if required. A hand signal means
it's your turn, then the current
pulls you in. Blood thrums in ears;

mind tells legs to stay put.
Yet you run, you point, you run
and hope your aim is true.
Run round corners and decide
in the half-moment it takes to squeeze
a trigger whether the starving, shattered man
in dusty rags is springing to attack
or raising hands in surrender.

Experience has taught you to squash
sudden movements like a niggling fly.
Survival instinct screams, "Engage!"
that genteel word that really means "Kill."
Stained teeth in a spurt of light.
Black smear on a wall. Stand
shaking in a cyclone of dust.
Later they will feed you the salve
of "collateral damage," which
will rip claws through your stomach's lining
for years to come. Now, though,
regret is a concept as foreign
as the land beneath your feet.

Long Live the Young Boys

Between cavalcades
of drumming thunder
and asphyxia, war
makes time for laughter.

Picture, if you will,
a shirtless gaggle of boys
on their backs,
warm breeze spraying sand,

stirring that youthful need
to cause trouble. Flak jackets
come off as "hurry up" shifts
to "wait." Machine guns

and rifles become teepees
in a field of brown
and fingers cock like pistols,
recalling days when killing

was bloodless and fun.
Pearson clutches his chest,
pirouettes, barrel-rolls
down a dune.

Sergeant Foust brays
like a donkey and Rambali
falls over, howling.
Pearson's form is still,

arms splayed, gap-filled teeth
goading lips into a smile
while laughter rains down
as if from Heaven.

From Above

It's how paratroopers see the world:
snapshot images before impact,
acquiring targets as we drift
on canopies of silk, death from above.

A lifetime ago in London
I rode a double-decker that
squeezed beneath low bridges.
Residents on sidewalks waved at
happy faces pressed to fogged glass.

Now, another two-story bus,
moves my platoon to its next
defensive position through
Riyadh's sandstone alleys.

Secrets unveil as we float
above clay parapets, soaring
past tiny girls playing soccer
without headscarves.

Our shadow is a serpent blotting
out sunlight, bristle of barrels
from windows the spiked armor
of a nightmare. Legs scamper,
tiny mouths throw shrieks at us.

I want to rain comfort
upon them like candy from
a parade float, want them
to stop and wave. But
I never lower my weapon.

Night Vision

Black dots intrude
on the green world
like ever-present
sand wriggling into

impossible places—
the spot beneath my armor
that rubs red welts
on flesh, sealed Ziploc bag

with pictures from home,
well-oiled bolt of my M16.
Vigilance is the cure.
Before every mission,

break down my weapon,
brush away grit, re-oil;
take a shower, wash away sins;
leave pictures behind,

squelch dreams of loved ones
witnessing such a foreign
version of their son,
brother, friend, lover.

In the shadow world
of static green, my mind
cannot dwell on such thoughts.
I must swim as the tide

that pulls my squad
inexorably forward
cascades through bolted
doors and sandstone hallways,

round corners that drip
with portent. Searching,
searching, always searching,
the pulsing spot from my

infrared illuminator dances
in the green. And when
it finds an obstacle
unwilling to let us pass,

there is a cure for that too.
The trigger knows the cure.
My finger knows, the green knows.
The green always knows.

Firing Pin

Gleaming sliver of silver,
size of a key.

One opens doors;
the other closes them.

Chemical Defense

In the desert, chemical alarms bray
with tinny music on the warm breeze.

We recall steel-chambered classrooms,
CS gas teaching lessons in a world

filled with fog. Soldiers dive into
rubber masks. Atropine injectors promise

renewed life if hearts seize, gift of time,
just enough for fingers to squeeze

triggers a few more times, before digits
become claws scratching at throats.

A test kits parses the air and everyone sweats
in charcoal-lined suits. Lowest-ranking man

is surrounded, weapons pointed at his feet.
He surrenders his rifle, lifts rubber edge

of a gas mask, inhales. Air seeps in
and seconds moan as we watch for twitches.

On the Road to Basra

Fleshy nubs wriggle on the boy's elbows,
forearms lost in stony plains of Al-Amarah
by a mine meant for Revolutionary Guards

then forgotten like the way he used
to twirl hair at the back of his neck
when he was three. Behind him

Saddam smiles on a sandstone wall, chest
festooned with medals. He doesn't realize
his face is pockmarked with bullet holes

and splashes of paint black as dried blood.
In the dusty courtyard, sandals kick a soccer ball.
One child breaks free from the scrum, dribbles

toward the crippled goalkeeper. The ball
sails past flailing stubs then bounces
back from the wall. Clapping elbows

together, the boy yells a taunt. His half-arms
dance above his head and he sets his jaw
as if to say, *Is that all you've got?*

Keepsake

Alarms ring out
from Riyadh's minarets
and eyes turn to the night sky.
A SCUD lumbers overhead,
an ostrich believing
it can fly. We've heard
the stories of Saddam using
chemical and biological agents
on his own people, but
orders forbid us from
unsealing our charcoal suits
until we cross Iraq's border.
When Patriots erupt
from batteries and race
to intercept, we gawk
like vacationers at
a fireworks display. Shrapnel
pings around us, gouges
asphalt instead of
soft, succulent flesh.
Sgt. Foust picks up a shard
shaped like a strip of bark.
It sizzles in the leather
fingers of his glove,
then rides in his cargo pocket
throughout the war.
Afterwards, he dumps it
in the bottom drawer
of his desk, jagged edges
slowly dulling beneath
the weight of routine.

Disinformation

The enemy attack has failed utterly. Allied soldiers are swimming in their own blood.

—Military communiqué broadcast over
Baghdad radio, Feb. 24, 1991

We practiced every detail,
even how to lie in letters
promising everything would be
all right. Briefings bled
with estimates of coming death,
mass casualty points
circled in grease pencil
on every map. In rehearsals,
soldiers heaved brothers
over shoulders, tried
not to think about
limp weight, what
that might presage.

When we crossed
the border and raced
toward Basra,
the radio announced
the airborne battalion
that jumped into Baghdad
had been annihilated. We,
the only paratroopers
in theater, knew better.
Little comfort, that,
for loved ones
half-a-world away
searching closets
for something
black to wear.

Ancient History

In Catholic school, we were told
the Euphrates was one of the rivers

of Paradise. In high school, the valley
of sand through which it flowed

became the cradle of civilization, birthplace
of Mesopotamia, Assyria, Babylon.

I didn't know what to expect when
I reached its banks, anything but this—

belching black of burning oil
blotting out a noontime sky.

A Clean Tool

Your weapon hasn't fired in days.
Still you clean it,
        give yourself,

to the task, everything
else shut
        out of your mind.

Yesterday is a far-off dream,
ripple of a rock skipped from
        a distant shore.

What is lost becomes invisible.
Eyes can't look back,
        ponder what this tool

has built, what it has torn down,
fingers fully occupied
        breaking down components.

A knuckle punches
a detent pin and receiver
        assembly opens like a mouth

hungry for silence. Feed it oil,
a swab pinched on
        a cleaning rod. Scrub soot

from barrel locking lugs.
Brush away sand,
        gunpowder, your sins.

Combat Art

My canvas is a brown landscape
begging for splashes of color.

My brush an M-16, 30-round clips
for tubes of paint, all of them red.

My subject wears a red-and-white
keffiyeh around his face,

tableau of him standing
in a white robe amid the rubble-strewn

street could be beautiful if not
for black hatred in his eyes.

Nights Like This

Nights like this
you wear your boots to sleep
knowing any moment
the cymbal crash of mortars
might intrude
upon your symphony of dreams.

Atop the cot
an unzipped sleeping bag wraps arms
around shoulders,
warmth of a lover whispering
in your ear,
soft lips kissing scarred skin.

It is enough
for quietude to breathe still air
in the land
of shuttered eyes, to massage
knotted knowledge
of all you have seen. And done.

Nights like this
you're not distracted by hard angles
of the rifle
sharing your bed, butt stock
pressed into ribs,
sling encircling your wrist like a noose.

While Others Sleep

Gunstock rests
atop sandbags

front sight post
thrust into darkness.

Condensation creeps
down plastic hand guards,

mesmerizingly slow,
tugging sentry's eyes

until his neck jerks.
Shivering beneath a

space blanket draped
over knotted shoulders,

bones crave comfort
of packed earth. But

it is his turn
to watch this sector,

protect against
nightmares come to life,

so he wipes away
moisture,

shrugs off
fog's caress,

becomes one
with the night.

At the Bottom of a Foxhole

We carry our world
in rucksacks, draw a line
in the sand, chests bared,

daring tanks to cross. Headlines
call us speed bumps,
promise gallons of death.

Pairs of men dig holes that might
become graves, reinforce
them with sandbags, then jump in.

At dusk, one stands tall to face
their sector of fire while the other
removes pictures of wife

and children from his helmet
to confess fears he dare not
whisper in light of day.

Understanding

Every soldier knows
his role, every cog
in the grinding,
gnashing machine.
To turn a life
into meat,
the green image
dancing in your scope
can hold no more
significance than
lint on your sleeve,
rolled off with tape
then discarded.

Finger poised
on a trigger
grows heavy
when eyes see
heart of a target.
Cards must be punched,
holes drilled. No time
for reflection.
Worry gives pause,
and spinning gears
don't care
whose hand they chew.

R. H. I. P.

Ask any private pouring diesel
into a barrel of human waste,

lighting it afire, mixing the stew
with a wooden paddle, standing

in the black smoke, he'll tell you:
Shit flows downhill. All one-stripes

on latrine duty know the motto:
Rank has its privileges. Nothing to do

but bitch to pals who are also
stuck in the muck. Unless you have

too many stripes, too much brass. Then
wants and grievances get shoved

in a cargo pocket, beneath maps and
Op-Orders, beneath everything olive drab.

Solitude is the true gift of rank. Voices
muffled behind camouflage.

Thunder in the Night

From the safety of sand-bagged bunkers
we listen to the thunderclaps of artillery
aimed at an enemy we hate but cannot see.
So easy to wage war this way, blind
to frightened looks of fathers clutching
family photos, kissing loved ones goodbye.

A C-130 rumbles through the clouds,
cocks its arm and hurls a twelve-ton bomb
at the desert. The punch lands miles away,
yet still squeezes our chests within its fist.
After 40 days of fire from the sky,
we cross the border to discover bodies
torn like waste paper passed through a shredder.
Pity tunnels toward our hearts, chewing holes
that, years later, will fill with acid every time
a storm brings thunder in the night.

Campaign Ribbons

Unit streamers shimmered like fire,
earned by forebears who crawled
across Omaha Beach.

How our young chests ached
for campaign ribbons of their own,
something bright and dazzling

on dress greens. Our armory
was a converted gym in Bedford,
a town that surrendered 19 of 30 boys

to French sand. Nineteen
plain stone crosses planted
on a grassy field

in Normandy.
I didn't know how much
each streamer cost

till I raced across
my own fields of sand,
witnessed death firsthand,

finally understood
why gold-fringed flags
are colored red.

Learning the Language

Our Arabic lessons come
from laminated cards,
vocabulary leached from
a headmaster's tongue:
Halt (a-QIF), Lie down (ag-LIS),
Drop your weapon
(da-a-si-LAHK ala-ess-FELL).

When Bedouins halt camels
near our column, we are speechless.
Mangos emerge from saddlebags.
They hold them to mouths,
then out toward us, beckoning.
Pantomime, the universal language.

A month I spent in France
was like this. Sixteen years old,
living with a family that spoke
no English. Pidgin French
ballooning like a Hawaiian shirt,
too big, too loud. Girls on
Cote D'Azur's topless beaches
giggled at my defective tongue.
Regarde comme ses joues sont rouge!
"Look how red his cheeks are!"

In the desert, Sergeant Foust
trades brown-sleeved MREs
then approaches a kneeling camel.
He swings a leg over its hump
and it rises like a piston, ass first.
The beast lurches through sand,
Foust clinging to fur,
the rest of us, Americans
and Arabs alike, laughing,
clapping each other on backs.

Quotas

Our company was allotted
six Bronze Stars, which
the C.O. said would go to
First Sergeant and officers,
himself included. He said it
as if he expected us to cheer.
We just sipped coffee
from frosted canteen cups,
leaned against Humvee hoods
for warmth. Desert nights
were surprisingly cold.

Nothing here went as expected.
Soldiers who buttoned
farewell letters in BDU pockets
before feeding themselves into
hungry mouths of bunkers
were greeted by starving men
wearing rags. Real danger lurked
in dark dunes that shook like
wet dogs, spraying cluster bombs
like fat, bloody ticks.

Hostilities were officially over,
but steel still filled
our nights. Civilians,
believing they were free,
rounded up, shot by Republican Guards.
Not our problem, the C.O. said.
One must compartmentalize.
What is right for us
need not be right for them.

Only six students may earn A's
no matter how many get
questions right; six tickets
in a patrolman's pad must
disappear by month's end;
and six Bronze Stars
will be pinned to puffed chests
while trigger pullers
stand nearby, saluting.

Ambush

In the suck we know what's expected.
Burrow into sand with nets draped
over heads to ward off flies from scalps.
A beige world that boils soldiers
while drifting dunes cough up
bombs and bodies torn in half.
Bury thoughts like dead comrades,
walk around in a skin that lies.

We fly home like lost boys emerging
from a dark forest after a night
of bitter cold. When our 747 lands,
we stow M-16s beneath seats
and offload the airliner unarmed,
unprepared for the ambush.

White-haired men stand at attention,
saluting, VFW caps bristling
with pins. In pinched creases
of their faces wallows the memory
of splashes of red paint, tie-dyed crowds
chanting *Baby Killers.*

God Bless the USA blares
from a deejay's speakers,
hands pat backs, lips buss cheeks.
Bright sundresses and Polo shirts
converge, swallow our column
of desert brown. Sand-blasted
dam finally cracks, levees break,
our world forever changed.

Blanket Party

In Basic Training,
you learn to keep
your mouth shut.

Answers other than
Yes, Drill Sergeant
earn punishment

for the entire
platoon. Low crawl
enough times

through sludge
and justice will come
after *Lights Out,*

when brown rounds
can plead ignorance.
Hands trap you

beneath a blanket
while your buddies
swing bars of soap

inside pillowcases
at your midsection.
Nothing broken.

Enough only
to bruise, enough
to teach a lesson.

Lessons from Panama

I.

Twenty-three years old, I knew it all—
combat patch on sleeve, airborne wings on chest.
On a Panama airstrip, two steps off the plane,
humidity coiled round my body, wrung
rivulets of sweat from my shirt. Infiltrating
the wall of green, we followed waddling anteaters
down sandy trails while they lapped up prey
like jelly beans and spider monkeys howled
from the steamy thatch: *Foolish men,*
we see you!

Night came darker than a crow's back. Vampire bats
swooped from canopy, crawled across jungle floor,
tasted soft flesh of trespassers, exchanging blood
for rabies. Snicking sounds of a million scissors
announced morning's arrival. A blanket of crabs
skittered from Atlantic shore to Pacific, their ten-foot swath
fluttering like a mile-long banner proclaiming
primal need to mate. We laughed and joked
from an armored cocoon as Humvee tires
cracked shells, crushed bodies.

II.

Our company commander took us to the Canal.
Water flowed from lock to lock, tossing cargo ships
as big as a high school like leaves
on a breeze, testament to what is possible
when mankind wants something. Even oceans
and continents can't stand in the way.

III.

Weekend pass in Panama City, armed with
American dollars and enough Spanish
to order *cervesas frias*. Inside the Marriott,
a shimmering oasis amidst
concrete-blocked tenements,
throngs of round-faced *señoritas* competed,
earnestly pressing bodies against GIs,
begging in broken English, *Pick me,*
make me yours, take me away.

Our rules were simple: dance, kiss,
promise, fuck. On the ride home
past squalid slums, try forgetting
plaintive eyes you leave behind.
From outside the bubble, the world
and its rules can be cruel; inside,
life is easy, especially
when you're twenty-three.

Things to do When You're Dead

Squadmembers' camouflaged backs
recede like pennies dropped
from a balcony. Their boots
continue without you,
each churning step
spitting puffs of sand.

> *Try to remember*
> *what was so important.*
> *Why the rush?*

The storm is over. Gunfire
gives way to distant shouts
from sergeants assembling
order from chaos.

> *Recall what it was like*
> *to be young, to lie in a field*
> *of clover, transform clouds*
> *into trains, buffalo, face*
> *of the first girl you kissed.*

Headcount is short one soldier.
Backtracking, they search for you...

> *Watch ants clamber up*
> *a date palm. How bristled*
> *its fibrous trunk, creaking*
> *as its green head shakes*
> *plaited fronds. Listen*
> *to whirring pulse of flies,*
> *give them your skin to explore.*

...but you're quiet as a coffin.

> Feel the world spin, sand
> massaging away your tension.
> Surrender your heat.
> Shiver. Wonder how long
> till you dissolve, till
> Earth reclaims its loan.

Particles

Nothing exists except atoms and empty space.

—Democritus

All smells are particulate. Think about that
as you march past burned trucks. Upon

melted seats are forms, blackened and shriveled
like banana peels left in the sun. Stench

wafts through your nose, tickles cilia,
lies down to sleep in your olfactory bulb.

A decaying piece of someone else.
A spot of liver. A morsel of tongue.

Only comfort is this: no one
ever dies; they simply change form.

Atoms that a day before
were my enemy, now my friend.

They wanted so much to escape.
I breathe deep, think, *Be with me.*

Aerodynamics

Pointed tips of bullets slice air
with supersonic cracks. Mortar
rounds hurl themselves from tubes,
fins providing grace to parabolas.

Bodies drifting on a breeze make easy
targets, so T-10s have no steering
lines. Paratroopers fall like
flowerpots knocked from ledges.

They rush to greet soil's fist
at 22 feet-per-second, impact
enough to snap straight legs
like fired clay. At the last second,

jumpers curl bodies like
runners on rocking chairs,
spread the kiss of earth from foot
to shoulder. Slink into tall grass.

Night Jumps

Bodies crammed together
in the belly of an iron whale
on a rough sea. Only light
is a red star burning

by the side door. Jumpmaster
runs a hand along its open mouth
as if caressing a lover's lips.
Propblast whips umbilical

as he scans black ink for a patch
of green. Paratroopers rise from
cargo seats, line up like pack mules.
Parachute, reserve, rucksack

on knees, weapon carrier
jammed beneath an arm.
Each jumper leans into next,
traces yellow static line

zig-zagging his back like bootlaces.
An error could mean the life
of the man in front, but trust
is an infant in a dark room.

When light turns green all boots
shuffle forward. Every second
another man steps to the cliff,
leaps, tastes the kiss of night air.

Red Legs

Like riding a bike:
scrape your knee

then get back on
right away.

And so the stick
reenters the belly

of a C-130
the next day.

No time to mourn
four from yesterday

now absent. We must
stand in the door

and leap without
wondering whether

trailing aircraft
are flying too low,

prop blades churning
like meat grinders.

Paratroopers are meant
to fall.

The Dead Aren't Allowed to Walk

Body bags aren't used
in training. A buddy
must heave dead weight
over a shoulder, haul it
like a sack of dog food.

Until found, the dead
must be mute, immobile.
Stones at the bottom of
a well, cold water seeping
into bones. Time waits
while they ponder
what will happen
when blanks become bullets.
When pumping hearts can be
silenced by twitch
of a finger.

At casualty points, the dead
reanimate. A warm tent
filled with cots and MREs.
The hanging sickle retreats
like a nightmare from daybreak.
Count how many play Spades
on overturned ammo cans.
It's almost like summer
vacation. Forgetting lessons
learned in school.

I Am a Soldier

I am son following father, brother
protecting his own. I am clay
sculpted by drill instructors
into muscled stature. A dog trained
to respond with gnashing teeth.
I am knowledge of all who humped
through sweating forests, slept
in muddy foxholes carved
into foreign soil. I am row of ribbons
on a starched uniform chest.

I am razored edge of sabers rattled
by fat politicians sheathed in Armani.
I am a chainsaw sent to prune.
I am tip of the spear thrust
into the side of Jesus. I am
a Devil in baggy pants.

I am both boogeyman and savior,
hand that feeds and hand
that takes away, calming palm
of soothing touch, fist
clenched in rage.

I am scent of cordite and wailing moans
that follow in my stead. I am clouds
of choking dust enveloping convoys
after IEDs explode. I am a liar
pressing plastic on a hissing chest,
promising everything will be all right.

I am metallic taste of fear, frothing mouth
of vengeance. I am red veil descending,
thousand-yard stare, violent outburst
at inappropriate times. I am a sullen wall
of silence, haunted dreams, sweaty nights.
I am the distant memory of a laughing boy.

II

Welcome Home

Yellow ribbons strangle trees
in the yard of my parent's home.
The first night back, friends

take me to a bar, pay
for all my drinks,
liquid tongue, the sweet kiss

of first love. Frank throws a party
at his father's house, gives me
the American flag they flew

while I was in Iraq. Shrugging,
I try to joke, and fail. One night
long ago, Frank's father

threw a tantrum because
I'd come over after midnight.
Such are the crises of suburbia.

His are not the screams I hear
as hands pat my back and
happy faces invade my space.

Breath should come easily.
Crowds aren't dangerous
in the land of plenty.

So smile, smile, enjoy the victor's
parade. There will be time
once lights go out

and minivans return to shade
of their own driveways to find
a safe corner in which to hide.

Love and War and Baking

My Georgia peach mailed
perfume-scented letters
promising sex, love,
and cookies—but mostly sex.
In heat of day, when we were
supposed to sleep, I'd stare
at her glossy, bikinied form.
Sultry smile and sidecast eyes
sending me to valleys
hot with moisture.

Reality never lives up
to dream's potential.
There were cookies, yes,
but that was all. Long ago
in Fort Benning's forests
our not-quite-love died,
gleaming skin peeling away
to reveal lack of seeds. But
the world is big, every turn
a road leading somewhere else.

And, of course, there were cookies.

Salvage

Sturdier than it appears,
the musician stands upon
spindly legs made from wire,

torso crafted from flattened
bullet casings. Even its
composition proclaims,

There is more to me
than meets the eye.
From detritus in our wake,

Bedouin artisans create
frozen moments of harmony.
Ignoring the howling

storms of this world,
the figurine strums
its wire guitar,

miniature crooning head
cocked to the sky.
Close your eyes,

you will hear not only
chords of blonde hair
and blue eyes, but the dusky

wail of a ney vibrating
in your chest, echoing
down to your DNA.

What I Remember About That Night

Smoke clinging to a dark nightclub ceiling
like steam off dry ice. Though I don't
really remember fog, this was before
smoking was outlawed. Before
cell phones and Internet. When people
had to talk to one another. Burning
eyes a small price for conversation.

Not that we could hear. Penguins
tilting in an Arctic gale, we clacked
into howls of house music.
Or maybe country or rock, I don't
recall. Only volume.
Everyone shouting in ears,
nodding at who knows what.

I was there with my war buddies,
three of them, a fire team clustered
at the bar. Fingernails scraped clean
of sand, palms flat on black lacquer,
texture the matted grip of congealed
blood. Or was the counter stainless steel,
as antiseptic as a morgue? Whichever,

we were ordering shots of tequila,
perhaps Goldschlager or Jaegermeister,
blasting our brains to obliterate
the crouching cells of memory.
Liquid shrapnel shredded buds
on our tongues. That's how we
did it, swallowing danger whole,
paying consequences in the morning.

And whether there were four of us,
or three, or just me and one other
high-and-tight gleaming amongst
the shags, we weren't drunk enough
to forget the smell of burning bodies.
I think I was the one who buried
my face in the perfumed cleavage
of the blonde, that valley of lavender
body wash. Who knows anymore?

Buddies either pulled her boyfriend
off me or I pulled him off one of them.
Whirlwind of bodies, a chair falling down,
then that blocky headed linebacker
offered up his chin and I connected
with my fist. Details fade, but not
the glossy patch of scarred skin
on my knuckles. Tattoo of brotherhood,
strand from an unraveling ball of yarn
to which I cling. Taste of blood
in my mouth, sound of it in my ears,
brothers standing for one another,
celebrating the fact we were alive.

Gathering Intel

Search the objective or kill zone
for casualties, documents, or equipment.

—Field Manual 7-8, Infantry Rifle Platoon and Squad

I didn't steal family photos
from the dead, but felt
no unease ripping
golden-eagled epaulets
from uniforms stained
with blood. Inside
a half-crushed bunker,
I found currency
stashed in a notebook
beside a bedroll. None
of what we found
was deemed important.
"Just keep it," they said,
so we did.

On the back of a purple
ten-dinar note, issued by
the Central Bank of Iraq,
a minaret is ringed with
mosaic etchings, garnished
rungs on a ladder to
heaven. Sometimes I
remove the bill from
its Ziploc bag and listen
for the wailing calls
of a muezzin leading
lost souls in prayer.

Begin Morning Nautical Twilight

*Begin morning nautical twilight (BMNT): The start of
that period where, in good conditions and in the absence of
other illumination, enough light is available to identify
the general outlines of ground objects and
conduct limited military operations.*

—Field Manual 101-5-1, Operational Terms and Graphics

Drop a rock into a stream
to alter its course, to change

the landscape, water will flow
around and over, continue as before.

Habits resist change. Take camouflage
jacket and pants from a soldier,

he will still wake before sunrise,
noiselessly search gloom

for movement, for targets,
for something to kill.

Desert Snapshots

Blue flame from a heat tab reflecting
off a private's dust-streaked face
as he heats a slurry of MRE components
in a canteen cup. The awe-struck expression
of a nineteen-year-old Skyping,
hunched over a computer screen,
finger-waving to the baby boy
his wife holds in her arms.

> *I store these images like Peter Pan's happy thoughts*
> *something to soothe bubbling acid on trips*
> *down anonymous dirt highways*
> *crowded with curbside litter.*

A platoon sergeant on one knee,
M-16 strapped to his back,
shaking the hand
of a four-year-old boy.
A puppy peeking from a cargo pocket,
tongue lolling, lanyard
of 550-cord looped
round its neck as a leash.

> *Best not to wonder what might be hidden*
> *in the rubble. The world can disappear*
> *in a clap of thunder, a whirlwind*
> *of sand and screams. Or else minutes*
> *will continue their slow march through*
> *shifting dunes and skirts of furrowed brown.*

A foursome in olive-drab tee shirts
playing Spades on overturned ammo cans.
Out of context, zooming in
so the wired vest and hand-held trigger
are out of frame, even the bomber's face
is beautiful, canted toward the sky,
eyes closed, lips parted in prayer.

Out of the Box, Almost

No more reveille, no push-ups
for stepping out of line. Boots
tied together, hanging from
a wire. Wake when I want,

wear a hat indoors, let hair
touch my ears. I can finally say
what I think about the President
without fear of a court martial,

do anything that enters my mind.
Leash gone, still I wait for a bell
at chowtime. Afraid to run free,
afraid of the invisible fence.

Transitive Property

When Alex was born nearly two months premature,
[Troy and Kelli Albuck] were told he might live only a few days
or even hours. On more than one occasion in the months following,
doctors called the Albucks to the hospital, believing Alex had only
a few hours to live. Miraculously, despite respiratory problems,
vision and hearing impairments, and a host of other ailments,
Alex recently celebrated his first birthday.

—Remarks by the Honorable Philip M. Crane to the
U.S. House of Representatives, March 1, 1994

"Have you heard about Troy's son?" Neal asks.
It always begins this way. First,
a voice from the past, then
the vortex pulling me into memory.

I conjure the image of four lieutenants,
barely of drinking age, holding AKs
and Dragonovs, standing on what looks like
the surface of the moon. Missing

from that picture is Troy, the lieutenant
from Delta Platoon attached to our company.
While we wormed through bunkers,
his HMMWVs guarded our flanks.

When we dug in, they sent him to
a captured ammo dump being rigged
to explode. Not until later did we learn
what munitions lived there.

Mushroom plume of sand and chemicals
one more ingredient to a sky
already black with oil. The tar pit
keeps coughing up bones. Agent Orange slept

for decades before touching my father
with its cancerous finger. Gulf War Syndrome
didn't wait as long, but Troy
was not the one to get sick.

Algebra's Transitive Property conveys
attributes from A to B to C. Who knew
variables could be human? Who knew
Troy's baby could pay for our ignorance?

Invisible

Everyone knows
about the dreaded knock,
an officer in blues

and a chaplain.
But few have
witnessed erasures.

We all see gleam
of silver trumpets, hear
"Taps" and soldiers

firing volleys, feel
fabric of a folded
flag pressed

into hands of a woman
dressed in black.
From this moment on

she is invisible, cast out
from base housing
before her shadow

can creep across
neighbors' lawns.
Moving vans steal away

beneath night's wing.
A new family appears,
greeted with smiles

and pies filled
with apples
and relief.

Hallowed Ground

"The Arts of War" by Leo Friedlander stands at the end of [Memorial Bridge]. In "Valor" on the left, the male equestrian is accompanied by a female striding forward with a shield; in "Sacrifice" a standing female symbolizing the Earth looks up to the rider Mars.

—National Park Service

Grand arched bridge spanning Potomac
unifying houses of Lincoln and Lee.
Tourists cross to granite walls with names
etched in blood. Gray-faced soldiers
clutch rifles, trudge through fields,
packs freighted with decisions
made beneath a dome they can't
quite see. Weary eyes scan
every direction, muscles tensing
each time foot touches ground.
But no one halts, each man ready
to surrender life for his brother. This,
they do in numbers far too great,
marching past golden gods of
Sacrifice and *Valor* to green hills
dotted with white stones. They drop
into black holes just as they've
been trained to do. Gloved hands
will salute, polished trumpets will blow.
Tourists will come and go. Grass
will continue to grow lush and green.

POWs

From the gloom
of my apartment
I sometimes hear
sandals shuffling
in the hallway
outside.

How many survived
after we sent them back
I do not know,
but if one knocks
on my door,
I will open it.

Reboot

All of us flew home,
taste of unfinished business
like chalk in our mouths.
Hard to accept
backslaps
when each touch
hearkened POWs
who shook our hands.
Before
we abandoned them.

Confusing, this
new war, but when
Saddam's statue
toppled and civilians
slapped his face
with their shoes,
for just one moment
I thought their glee
might be enough
to change history.

Get Some

They chant it, these zombies
clutching joysticks, mesmerized
by screens of pulsing light, splashes
of color. *Get some. Get some.*
Cave dwellers wearing headsets.
Avatars run, point, shoot
at friends whose faces
they've never seen.
Get some. Get some.

Sunshine is no lure. No excitement
in swatches of green grass.
No wonder in the sky.

They want to know what it's like
to watch a head explode in real life.
Can't wait till they are 18, worried
they'll miss their chance to
Get some.

I want to roll a boulder
into their river, change
its course. I want to press
weight of history upon them.
But their minds are already flat.

They howl at videos of skateboarders
faceplanting, grinding tracts
of skin on pavement.
Whoa, dude, he got him some!

These boys wear innocence
like a dirty diaper. If only
I could shield their eyes
before jigsaw of someone
they once knew

burns into retinas. Before nostrils
fill with charred flesh,
eardrums reverberate with yowls
for help, cries for mama.

I want to pound the pain of yesterday
so deep into their chests
that they'll be careful tomorrow.
If they knew how soft a body
really was, would that lessen
their love of steel? Would they
caress their arms and legs
to savor the memory? Or would they
still want to *Get some*?

Imagine, I want to say, a nail
piercing your foot s l o w l y,
rusted barbs ripping raw edges
of flesh. Multiply that by a hundred.
By a thousand! But these kids
are not good at math. They will live forever.
They will *Get some*. Taste it
for themselves. Taste it, smell it,
chew it, swallow it. Become what
they've dreamed of since weaning
off cartoons. *Get some! Get some! Get some!*
The mantra spews and only one thing
will salve this slash of longing,
one cure, one blade that promises
exactly what they want.

The guillotine beckons and up
the steps they climb, chanting
with each footfall, *Get some. Get some.*
To look inside its basket, they must
expose tender necks. Even this
won't stop them. Nothing will.
Not until they *Get some, Get some.*
Until they *Get some.*

Like My Father Flies

I.

In Vietnam, my father dropped bombs,
dodged missiles big as telephone poles.
His stories remained locked behind mute lips,
one of many lessons taught by example.

On Air Force bases overseas, my childhood
homes stood next to runways. Dad ate
dinner in a flight suit, kit bag lurking,
a landmine by the door. Pecking, we'd wait
for the wall-mounted speaker to squawk its alert,
yank him from our meal. When night's maw
swallowed him, I would chew the question
no one dared voice: *Was it just another drill?*

II.

His F-4 wore camouflage on its body,
a shark's mouth on its nose. After school,
I, too, dressed up, donned black boots,
green gloves, g-suit with compression leggings,
reverently touched unit patches on hallway plaques.

Sons of pilots rode bikes together, parked
at runway's end while Phantoms roared,
ripped the blue like lightning. From bomb shelters'
concrete curves, we jumped into mountains
of leaves, shouted *Geronimo,*
pretended we could fly.

III.

Pilots don't wear glasses. I have my mother's eyes,
vision too poor to drive at night. I became, instead,
a paratrooper, jumping from cargo planes
that rumbled like buses through gray skies.
Floating beneath a silk canopy:
closest I could come to being him.

IV.

These days I wander country roads, pause
to examine seedlings struggling
to break the bonds of Earth, stretching
toward the sun. When jets slice sky
into white contrails, I slit my eyes
until the world on which I walk
is nothing but a blur.

And I am flying.
I am flying.
Flying.

Hardship Tours

Too young to worry when
Daddy dropped bombs
in Vietnam. A toddler learning
to walk. Only later did I think
of Mom raising three kids
on her own, fearing the front door
for what a knock might bring.

Ten years later, he went to Iran.
Acid finally burned my stomach.
Ayatollah Khomeni barking
on nightly news, my mother
learning to smoke. That was the year
I gave up playing piano,
began to think I was a man.

When my time came, I entered a plane
in desert fatigues, eager to tread
same ground as Daddy's boots.
Parents waving goodbye from
the tarmac. Just the second time
my mother saw my father cry.

Good with Hands

I wasn't good with hands until
I joined the Army. Never learned
to take apart toasters and lamps,
run wiring through a wall.
Changing oil or a flat
the only tools in my box.

A drill instructor took
soft clay and sculpted
iron fists. I learned
to cradle a neck
in the crook of my elbow,
drop so the skull snaps
free from spine.
To conceal sharp edge
of a bayonet against
my forearm before slicing.
To swing back and strike
the sweet spot.

When the war ended
and we were told to put away
our toys, I was glad to see
a drunk push his wife.
Hands free once more
to do their job, block
slow punches, break
a lip, close one eye
behind a swollen cheek.
Gather all my blood
and proclaim
that I am good
for something.

Age of Consent

Easy to forget how young I was
when asked to kill or be killed.

The past is a window caked with
ashes of spent years. Tutankhamen

clasped his first golden scepter
at ten. Released it at nineteen.

Framed by a striped Nemes headdress,
face on his sarcophagus is confident,

wiser than time. Our own pyramids
were built atop new recruits fresh

from high school, more comfortable
holding a rifle than a razor. Wars

are always fought by children. A kid,
once dared, will leap from a rooftop

into a pool. Regret is a word
in dictionaries of old men.

Skin Hunger

In World War II, orphan babies
slipped quietly into night,
"Failure to Thrive" written on
their charts. A gentle touch
was all it took to wrest them
from death's clutch. Nurses
soon learned, cradled
infants in warm arms,
cuddled, gave them
reason to live.

Now our world is united by
digital superhighways,
where four-way chats
between L. A., New York,
London, and Beijing
occur in real time,
yet still we fail to thrive,
melancholy creeping over us
one keystroke at a time
as we retreat from neighbors
to live in virtual reality
so nearly complete,

all that's missing
is the human touch.

Prepare to Land

After you have slipped into the wind, you will assume a landing attitude by keeping your feet and knees together, knees slightly bent, with your head and eyes on the horizon.

—FM 3-21.220, Static Line Parachuting Techniques and Tactics

One time I jumped
from a helicopter,
a disposable camera

attached by 550-cord
to a belt loop.
Against procedure, of course,

for there were other things
to do—lower equipment
at 200 feet AGL, slip

into wind at 100. All lost
as I fell to Earth,
a winter leaf

remembering spring.
I tossed the camera,
but instead of dropping

out of sight, the tiny box
hovered at my waist.
Buffeted by wind, it danced

and I followed.
Years later, still I float
mesmerized,

waiting for ground
to come up
and hit me.

Range Practice

I practiced what to say while you
stomped about the kitchen,
slamming dishes and cabinets.

Just like range practice, I focused
on the target, took air slow as a turtle,
emptied my heart. Practice doesn't always

make perfect. Punching holes downrange
easy when the torso bisected by
your front sight post isn't breathing.

Lines rehearsed without emotion
seldom survive first contact.
Paper targets don't fire back.

On Dying

I.

Giant pine outside window of my youth,
guardian with sturdy limbs skimming
clouds while my bones crackled
through growth spurts. Each spring,
it spoke the promise of color.

When lightning stabbed the Earth,
I huddled on my bedroom floor, lungs filled
with static, cochlear hairs singed
and bent. Bright scar burned into bark,
thin lips whispering, *Death*
is always close. Anywhere you hide,
its bleached bone hand can wrap
fingers round your throat.

II.

The Army taught me how to kill:
rifles at a distance, hand-to-hand
combat at close quarters. In sawdust
pits we screamed our credo—
Kill! Kill! Kill!—lunged with bayonets,
learned to snap a neck, thrust a knife.
Before we crawled beneath
poncho liners, we killed chiggers
burrowing in our skin, smothered them
with acetone. Annihilation all we knew.

III.

The tree was dead but didn't know;
lightning's lingering bite eating
her core, erasing the past ring by ring.
She colored one more spring
with green, embraced the wind.

I, too, ignored the black dog curled
round my feet. My heart seemed safe
in its quiet tomb. How was I to know
it had ceased to beat?

Echoes

She's saying something about a show
on HGTV; someone has traded spaces

or simply invaded another's. But
my mind is in the desert. With gunfire.

Explosions. Plumes of dust.
Her lips move up and down,

voice muffled as if coming
from a closed coffin. If only

life were as simple as
a remodeling show. She could

spackle, splash color, bend
the world to her design,

while I accept whatever
changes greet my return.

How to Disappear

First, bring home memories
caked with sand, enough
to build a bunker. Then hide
from light and air. Springtime
will slip from memory
once green hills turn brown.

Ignore shimmer at edges
of blinds, the tantalizing
kiss of blue sky. Recall
what lurks inside black clouds.
Turn the locked door into
a barricade against monsters
scratching at the keyhole.

Listen to pipes beneath a sink
that holds one plate,
one cup, one spoon.
A roiling echo will
call to mind sharks
circling a doomed life raft.

When others offer help,
press lips together,
look away. Delete messages
unheard. Count breaths.
Stand as still as framed photos.
Blend in with wallpaper.
Gather dust.

Like the slow erasure of rock
succumbing to dripping water,
you won't realize
you've disappeared
until everyone else
stops looking.

Glossary

550-cord: All purpose nylon cord favored by the military.

AGL: Above ground level.

Air Assault: A mission where troops enter the battlefield by helicopter insertions.

Airborne: A mission where troops and/or equipment enter the battlefield by parachute drop.

BDU: Battle-Dress Uniform. Refers to military camouflage uniforms.

BMNT: Begin Morning Nautical Twilight. The period just before dawn when approaching sunlight reflects off the atmosphere and provides dim illumination. This has long been held to be the optimal time to conduct attacks, when the enemy might still be asleep and you have enough light to see what you're doing.

Brown Round: Nickname for a drill sergeant; drill sergeants are the only military members who wear the iconic campaign hat, which is brown with a large, round brim.

C-130: A cargo plane with four propeller driven engines. This and the C-141 are the standard airplanes for airborne operations.

Cervesas fria: Spanish for cold beer.

CO: Commanding Officer.

CS Gas: Crowd Suppressant gas. The military version of tear gas.

Court Martial: A military court proceeding.

Dishdasha: Long white robes commonly worn in the Middle East.

F-4: Vietnam-era Air Force jet. Called a Phantom.

FM: Field Manual. The official "how-to" book for a particular military operation.

Front sight post: The front aiming post on an M-16 rifle.

Guide-on: The rod or staff holding a unit's flag and banners.

High-and-Tight: A military haircut that leaves hair only on the crown of the head, giving the shaved sides a shiny appearance.

Humvee: Phonetic for HMMWV (High-Mobility Multipurpose Wheeled Vehicle). An all-terrain, four-wheel drive, military vehicle. A Hummer.

IED: Improvised Explosive Device. A bomb culled from whatever is readily available.

Jumpmaster: The paratrooper in charge of airborne operations aboard a particular plane.

Keffiyeh: A Middle Eastern scarf.

KIA: Killed In Action.

M-16: Standard-issue automatic rifle for US military.

M-60: Heavy US machine gun. Nicknamed "the pig." It fires a heavier round than the M-16, is belt-fed, and uses a three-man team for firing: the gunner, the assistant gunner (the man who feeds the belt into the gun), and the ammo bearer.

MOPP: Mission-Oriented Protective Posture. Refers to gas masks and the charcoal-lined suits with rubber gloves and boots that soldiers wear to protect themselves from chemical and biological contaminants.

Movement to Contact: A tactical movement in a general direction or toward a given location when enemy contact is expected or desired.

MRE: Meal Ready to Eat. Field rations that come in dark brown pouches, which are labeled by the main meal contained within. Also included are crackers, peanut butter, cocoa powder, coffee, creamer, salt, pepper, and a dessert.

Ney: A ney is a wooden Persian flute consisting of a hollow cylinder with finger holes. Its origins date back 5000 years, making it one of the oldest musical instruments still in use today.

OPORD/Op Order: Operations Order. This is the designated five-paragraph structure for information about a new mission to be disseminated via the chain of command. It provides information on (1) Situation, (2) Mission, (3) Execution, (4) Support, and (5) Command and Control.

Overwatch: A position from which an individual or team provides supporting or covering fire for another individual or team that is moving.

Patriot Missile System: A surface-to-air missile designed used in the Gulf War to intercept and destroy incoming SCUD missiles.

POW: Prisoner of War.

Propblast: air discharged behind a propeller-driven engine.

Receiver Assembly: One of the four main components of an M-16. The four components are: (1) upper receiver assembly, (2) lower receiver assembly, (3) bolt and bolt carrier assembly, and (4) magazine group assembly.

Republican Guard: Elite Iraqi military unit during Saddam Hussein's rule.

Reveille: A morning wake-up song usually played by bugle.

Revolutionary Guards: A branch of the Iranian military with a dual purpose of defending Iran's borders and protecting the country's Islamic system. Iran's Revolutionary Guards invaded Iraq numerous times over the eight years of the Iran-Iraq war.

R.H.I.P.: Rank Has Its Privileges.

SAW: Squad Automatic Weapon. A belt-fed, light machine gun. It fires the same size round as an M-16.

SCUD: A tactical ballistic missile developed by the Soviet Union during the Cold War.

Slip: During a parachute drop, a paratrooper will "slip" into the wind at 100 feet AGL. This means he will pull down on the two risers (straps) opposite the direction the wind is blowing. This will cant the dome of the parachute backwards to create slightly more drag and slow him down just before impact.

Static line: The yellow, nylon cord that connects a parachute to a cable inside an airplane. When a paratrooper jumps out, this cord will deploy his parachute. The end of the cord inside the parachute is connected by rubber bands that snap away from the force of the dropping body.

Stick: A group of paratroopers aboard an individual plane.

Acknowledgments

Grateful acknowledgements are due to the editors of the following publications where these poems have appeared, sometimes in slightly different form:

American Society: What Poets See: "Invisible"
Barely South Review: "Night Jumps"
The Chaffey Review: "I Am a Soldier"
Chiron Review: "Skin Hunger"
Clinch Mountain Review: "Campaign Ribbons" and "Red Legs"
Common Ground Review: "The Dead Aren't Allowed to Walk"
Comstock Review: "Good with Hands"
Connecticut River Review: "Ambush" and "Aerodynamics"
First Literary Review—East: "Out of the Box, Almost"
Illya's Honey: "Prepare to Land"
Narrative Magazine: "Combat Art," "From Above," "Half a Man," and "Particles"
New York Quarterly: "Lessons from Panama"
Poet Lore: "Gathering Intel"
Proud to Be: Writing by American Warriors: "Clearing a Room," "Desert Moon," and "Search Team"
Red River Review: "Echoes"
Spillway: "Firing Pin"
Sweetbay Review: "On Dying" and "Thunder in the Night"
Tampa Review Online: "Range Practice" and "R. H. I. P."

Special thanks are due to Ann Shalaski, Terry Cox-Joseph, and Carolyn Kreiter-Foronda, who each gave encouragement and advice throughout the long process of revision. Thank you for being so vicious with your pen and so loving with your comments.

Cover photo of the author by a platoon member; back cover author photo by Dawn Sullivan West; cover and interior book design by Diane Kistner (dkistner@futurecycle.org); Chaparral Pro text with Foobar Pro titling

About FutureCycle Press

FutureCycle Press is dedicated to publishing lasting English-language poetry and flash fiction books, chapbooks, and anthologies in both print-on-demand and ebook formats. Founded in 2007 by long-time independent editor/publishers and partners Diane Kistner and Robert S. King, the press incorporated as a nonprofit in 2012. A number of our editors are distinguished poets and writers in their own right, and we have been actively involved in the small press movement going back to the early seventies.

The FutureCycle Poetry Book Prize and honorarium is awarded annually for the best full-length volume of poetry we publish in a calendar year. Introduced in 2013, our Good Works projects are devoted to issues of universal significance, with all proceeds donated to a related worthy cause. Our Selected Poems series highlights contemporary poets with a substantial body of work to their credit. Our flash fiction line presents quick reads that can be serious or light-hearted, irreverent or quirky, fantastic or futuristic, or just plain fun.

We are dedicated to giving all of the authors we publish the care their work deserves, making our catalog of titles the most diverse and distinguished it can be, and paying forward any earnings to fund more great books.

We've learned a few things about independent publishing over the years. We've also evolved a unique, resilient publishing model that allows us to focus mainly on vetting and preserving for posterity the most books of exceptional quality without becoming overwhelmed with bookkeeping and mailing, fundraising activities, or taxing editorial and production "bubbles." To find out more about what we are doing, come see us at www.futurecycle.org.

The FutureCycle Poetry Book Prize

All full-length volumes of poetry published by FutureCycle Press in a given calendar year are considered for the annual FutureCycle Poetry Book Prize. This allows us to consider each submission on its own merits, outside of the context of a contest. Too, the judges see the finished book, which will have benefitted from the beautiful book design and strong editorial gloss we are famous for.

The book ranked the best in judging is announced as the prize-winner in the subsequent year. There is no fixed monetary award; instead, the winning poet receives an honorarium of 20% of the total net royalties from all poetry books and chapbooks the press sold online in the year the winning book was published. The winner is also accorded the honor of being on the panel of judges for the next year's competition.

Made in the USA
Charleston, SC
19 October 2013